BIRDS

Modern-Day Dinosaurs

Kerri O'Donnell

The Rosen Publishing Group, Inc.
New York

Published in 2001 by The Rosen Publishing Group, Inc.
29 East 21st Street, New York, NY 10010

Book Design: Haley Wilson

Photo Credits: Cover, pp. 2–3, 7, 14, 16–19, 22–24 © Linda Hall Library; pp. 1, 4–5 © Stockbyte; pp. 8–9 © Linda Hall Library/ © John Taylor/FPG International; pp. 10–11 © Telegraph Colour Library/FPG International; pp. 12–13 © Stockbyte/© Tom McHugh/National Museum of Natural History/© Peabody Museum/© Linda Hall Library; pp. 20–21 © Chris Butler/Science Photo Library; p. 22 © O. Louis Mazzatenta/National Geographic.

ISBN: 0-8239-8170-3
6-pack ISBN: 0-8239-8572-5

Manufactured in the United States of America

Contents

There's a Dinosaur in My Backyard!

Your little brother runs into the house and says, "Hey, I just saw a dinosaur!" Do you believe him? Maybe you should. Your little brother might not be making it up.

Most scientists think that all the dinosaurs died about 65 million years ago. For a long time, scientists believed that when the dinosaurs disappeared from Earth, they did not leave behind any traces of themselves. Today, scientists believe that the **relatives** of dinosaurs are alive and well.

The birds that you see in your own backyard may be the relatives of dinosaurs!

Step outside and look up in the sky or in a nearby tree. If you see a bird, you may be looking at the relative of a dinosaur!

Scientists have spent years studying dinosaur **fossils**. After the dinosaurs died, sand and mud covered their bodies. Over millions of years, the sand, mud, bones, teeth, and footprints became rock. These rocks are fossils. Scientists can compare dinosaur fossils to living animals, like birds.

Scientists believe that birds came from dinosaurs because of the common **traits**, or features, that birds and dinosaurs share. Some scientists even call birds "living dinosaurs."

Scientists study fossils like this one from 150 million years ago to learn more about dinosaurs.

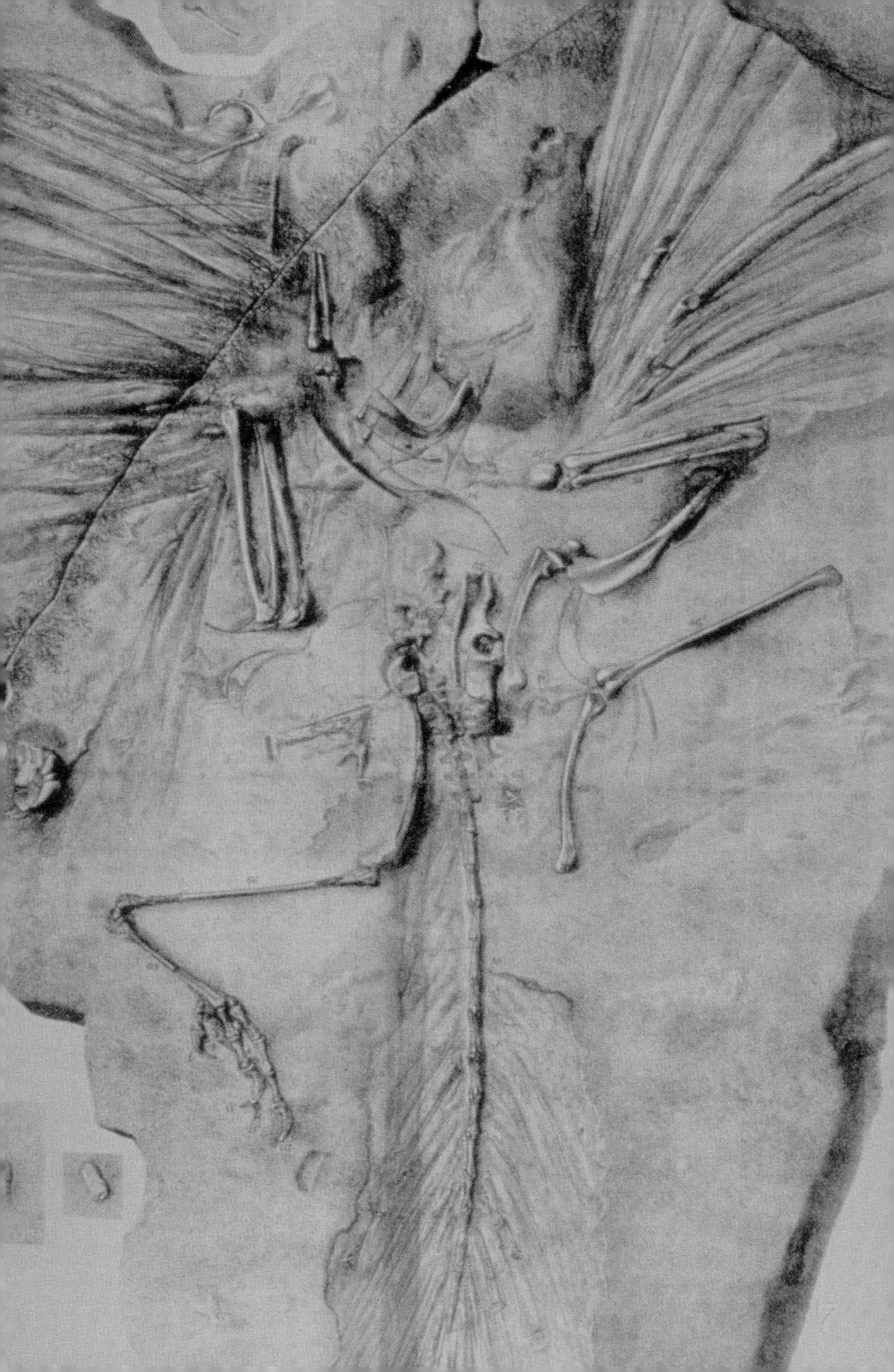

The Story of the Dinosaurs

Dinosaurs lived on Earth for 165 million years. Scientists have found fossils from over 450 different kinds of dinosaurs. Diplodocus (duh-PLAHD-uh-kus) lived around 150 million years ago in what is now the western United States. Diplodocus was almost as long as three school buses parked end to end. Stegosaurus (steg-uh-SOR-us) lived in the same area around the same time. Stegosaurus had sharp tail spikes and hard plates on its back to keep itself safe from enemies. Saltopus (sal-TOP-us) lived 220 million years ago, and was smaller than a house cat!

Large, powerful dinosaurs like the stegosaurus ruled Earth until about 65 million years ago.

Scientists believe that an asteroid caused changes on Earth that killed off the dinosaurs.

Scientists believe that an **asteroid** from space crashed into Earth about 65 million years ago. They think this asteroid made a huge **crater** in the Gulf of Mexico. Some scientists believe that a volcano **erupted** around the same time in what is now India.

These events sent a lot of smoke and dust into the air, which blocked out sunlight for months all over Earth. No sunlight and very cold **temperatures** made plants die, and food became almost impossible to find. Without plants, plant-eating dinosaurs starved. Meat-eating dinosaurs starved because there were no plant-eating dinosaurs left to eat. It is likely that these changes killed off most of the dinosaurs.

How Dinosaurs Changed Over Time

The first dinosaurs lived about 225 million years ago. Over millions of years, the dinosaurs went through a slow **process** of change. Dinosaurs with different traits began to **develop**. Some dinosaurs had traits that helped them live for a long time. Other dinosaurs had traits that did not help them. These dinosaurs gradually died out.

This process happened for all of the creatures that live on Earth today. It is happening all the time. It takes millions of years, so the changes are impossible for us to see.

Over millions of years, a dinosaur like this one may have become a lot like the birds we see today.

Stegosaurus

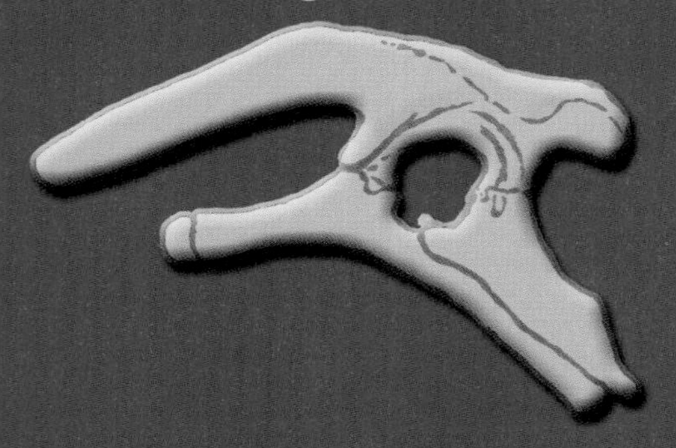

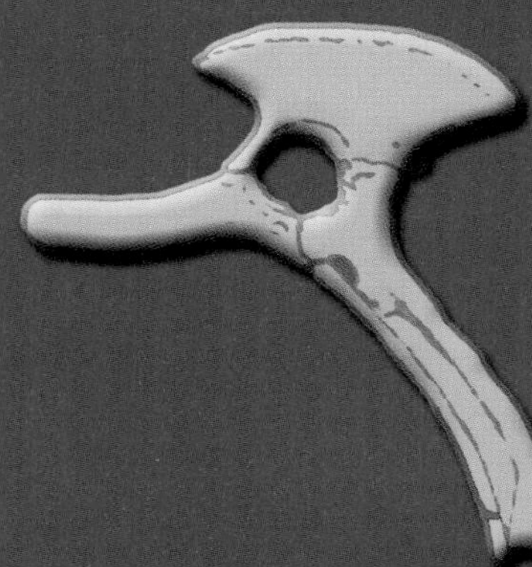

Allosaurus

Morosaurus

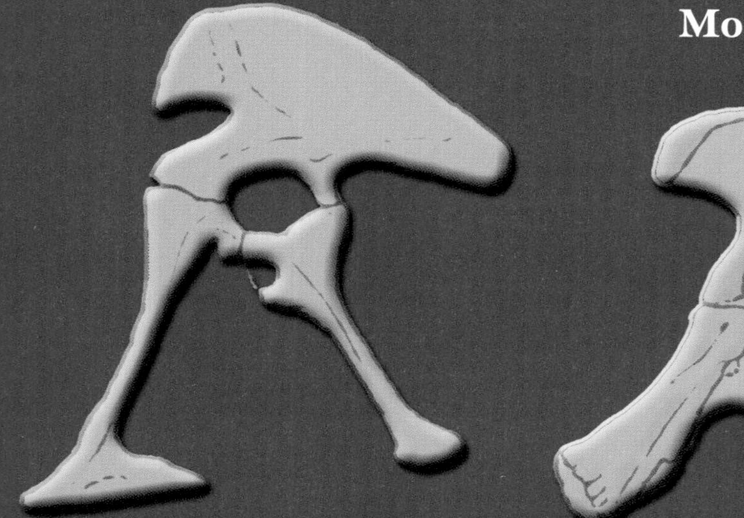

A Close Look at Bones

Scientists look closely at the things that are the same between different animals. This helps them decide which animals are related to one another.

When scientists looked at birds, they saw some interesting things. They discovered that birds have a lot in common with dinosaurs. All dinosaurs had a hole in their hip **socket**, where the leg bone connects to the main part of the body. Birds have this same hole! This led scientists to believe that birds and dinosaurs may be related.

The hip sockets were the same even among dinosaurs with different body types.

Scientists made another discovery about birds and dinosaurs. The bones of birds are hollow, just like the bones of dinosaurs were. Tyrannosaurus rex (tih-ran-uh-SOR-us REKS) had hollow bones. This huge dinosaur was a type of dinosaur called a **theropod**. Theropods were the only meat-eating dinosaurs, and they came in all sizes. Tyrannosaurus rex grew to be about forty feet long! Other theropods were much smaller. No matter what their size, all theropods had hollow bones, just like birds.

For a long time, scientists thought that birds had developed hollow bones so their bodies would be lighter for flying. Now we know that hollow bones were around in dinosaurs long before birds ever existed.

Tyrannosaurus rex was a theropod with hollow bones. Today's birds have hollow bones too!

One type of theropod, called a maniraptor (MAN-ih-rap-ter), was much smaller than tyrannosaurus rex. Maniraptors had a special bone in each wrist that was shaped like a half-moon. Guess which kind of animals today have this same wrist bone. That's right—birds do!

So far, we have three major clues that birds are related to dinosaurs:

- Birds have the same hole in their hip sockets that all dinosaurs had.
- Birds have hollow bones like theropods had.
- Birds have a special wrist bone like maniraptors had. This wrist bone is needed for flight.

This maniraptor's curved wrist bone is like the wrist bone found in birds today.

A Bird's Relatives

Two relatives of the first bird were maniraptors. These maniraptors were called velociraptor (vuh-LAH-suh-RAP-ter) and deinonychus (dy-NAHN-ih-kus). Velociraptor was about six feet long and three feet tall. This dinosaur ran quickly and close to the ground as it chased its **prey**. Velociraptor had sharp claws on its hands and feet for catching prey, much like hawks and eagles do today.

Deinonychus also ran quickly and hunted the same way that velociraptor did, using its claws to catch its prey. They looked alike, too. Both of these dinosaurs had a Y-shaped bone called a wishbone in the center of their chests, just like most modern birds do.

Velociraptor and deinonychus were both small but deadly. They had long, sharp claws that they used to catch their prey.

Fossil Finds

In 1999, fossils of protarchaeopteryx (proh-TAR-kee-OP-ter-iks) were found in China. This dinosaur had feathers, but it couldn't fly. It probably had feathers to keep warm.

Archaeopteryx (ar-kee-OP-ter-iks) lived about 150 million years ago. It had jaws and teeth instead of a beak, but it had feathers that were a lot like the feathers of today's birds. Archaeopteryx probably used its feathers to keep warm and maybe to fly short distances. Scientists believe it was the first bird.

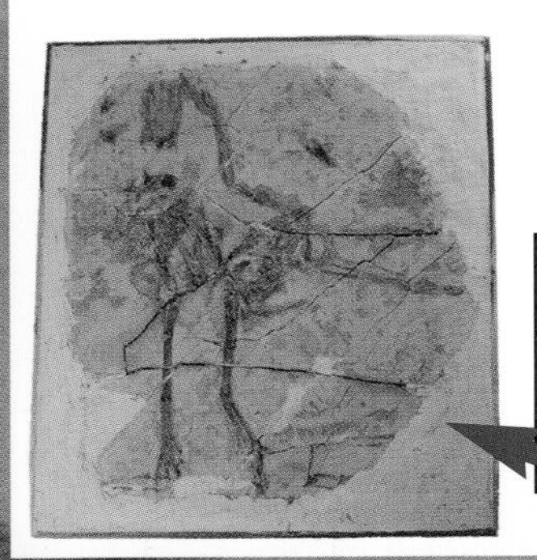

This fossil of protarchaeopteryx is very important in studying how dinosaurs and birds are related.

Glossary

asteroid A rock-like object found in space.

crater A hole in the ground shaped like a bowl.

develop To change gradually.

erupt To burst or flow.

fossil The hardened remains of a dead plant or animal.

prey An animal that is eaten by other animals for food.

process The gradual changes that lead to a certain outcome.

relative A member of a family.

socket An opening or hole meant to hold something.

temperature How hot or cold something is.

theropod A type of dinosaur that had hollow bones like modern birds.

trait A special feature.

Index